Gratitude
A Journal of the Heart

In Appreciation

To my family and the women who came before me and guided me with their
unconditional love, their triumphs and their tribulations: my grandmother, my mom,
my aunt and my great aunt. Thank you for your courage, your strength and your passion
for life! You truly have been and continue to be an inspiration.

Thank you Terri Mudd for planting the seeds of gratitude in my heart! My thanks to
Leslie Zemsky for making the dream a reality. Thank you Karen Ely and Sylvia Somerville
for being the wind beneath my wings and encouraging me to bring this journal to the
world. Thank you Jane Perini, who miraculously brought the journal to life and added all
the special touches that make it a professional work of art. My heart is overflowing
with a tremendous amount of gratitude that is immeasurable!

© Natalie Hoerner 2019
Gifts of Gratitude
ISBN: 978-0-9861602-5-7

Natalie is available to speak at or facilitate workshops and retreats.
Please contact her at: gifts-of-gratitude.com

Cover and book design: thundermountaindesign.com

Quotation by Mother Teresa: The writings of Mother Teresa of Calcutta © by the
Mother Tesesa Center, exclusive licensee throughout the world of the Missionaries
of Charity for the works of Mother Teresa. Used with permission.

A portion of the proceeds from the sale of this book will be
given to local children's charities of Buffalo, New York.

Gratitude
A Journal of the Heart

Created by Natalie Hoerner
with illustrations by Leslie Zemsky

Gratitude means being thankful, counting our blessings,
and being aware of all the goodness and beauty that surrounds us.
Gratitude is a simple exercise that has a great impact on our lives.
It shifts our focus from what we lack to the gifts we already have.
Research proves that gratitude, when practiced regularly, increases
our happiness and health. This is my wish for you!

I would love to hear what gratitude has done for you!
Please email me at: natalie@gifts-of-gratitude.com

The quotes in this journal have been collected over the years,
with hope that they are correct in content and author.

INTRODUCTION

Just before Thanksgiving in 2010, I came across an article in the *Buffalo News* by a woman named Terri Mudd. "Gratitude Journal Reveals Great Wealth" went straight to my heart, and I knew my life would never be the same. I became compelled by an idea that I could not let go of—to create some kind of gratitude journal for myself and others. Right away, I began asking everyone I knew if they had any thoughts about how I might make this a reality.

Finally Leslie Zemsky, a local artist and friend, helped me to set in motion a year-long process of developing my first gratitude journal. The creative journey was capped off with a dinner party for family and special friends around Christmas time, where I gifted a beautiful edition of the journal to everyone there. It was a kind of legacy piece for me since it contained special quotes and poems I had collected and saved over many years. I felt a part of my heart was truly captured in it.

Reading Terri Mudd's article was the start of not only what you are holding in your hands today but also of a life recreated. Through my little "Gratitude Journal that could," a surprising series of coincidences, chance meetings and miracles occurred. And I am forever grateful for all the places I went, the courses I took, and the people I met. In fact, I am sure I could write a book about those adventures alone!

Gratitude: A Journal of the Heart is the next iteration of my gratitude journal, reimagined from all the richness the first one afforded me. I intuitively followed the inspiration Terri provided me, and it opened up my world and miracles continue to unfold. From friends and family who received the original journal, I have come to realize that we should never doubt that we can make a positive difference in the lives of others.

So please enjoy and use this journal. My sincere hope is that it helps you find the inspiration and joy to put your dreams out into the world too!

Gratitude is the fairest blossom which springs from the soul.

HENRY WARD BEECHER

Whenever we are appreciative, we are filled with a sense of well-being and swept up by the feeling of joy.

M.J. Ryan

*If we make our goal to live a life of compassion
and unconditional love, then the world will
indeed become a garden where all kinds
of flowers can bloom and grow.*

ELISABETH KÜBLER-ROSS

ROY BENNETT

He is a wise man who does not grieve for things which he has not,
but rejoices for those which he has.

EPICTETUS

Let us be grateful to people who make us happy,
they are the charming gardeners who make our souls blossom.

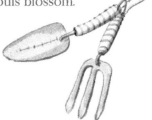

MARCEL PROUST

To everything there is a season, a time for every purpose under heaven.

ECCLESIASTES 3:1

Gratitude
makes sense of our past,
brings peace for today,
and creates a vision for tomorrow.

MELODY BEATTIE

*Someone's sitting in the shade today
because someone planted a tree long ago.*

- WARREN BUFFETT

Many people will walk in and out of your life,
but only true friends will leave footprints in your heart.

ELEANOR ROOSEVELT

Just when the caterpillar thought the world was over, I became a butterfly.

PROVERB

Our true home is in the present moment.
To live in the present moment is a miracle.

THICH NHAT HANH

The past is history. The future is a mystery. But today is a gift of God, that's why they call it the present.

BIL KEANE

*When one has
a grateful heart,
life is so beautiful.*

ROY T. BENNETT

Happiness is the spiritual experience of living every minute with love, grace and gratitude.   DENIS WAITLEY

A journey of a thousand miles must begin with a single step. CHINESE PROVERB

BE MINDFUL.

BE GRATEFUL.

BE POSITIVE.

BE TRUE.

BE KIND.

ROY T. BENNETT

Gratitude is not only the greatest of virtues,
but the parent of all others.

MARCUS TULLIUS CICERO

The best and most beautiful things in the world cannot be seen or even touched—they must be felt with the heart.

HELEN KELLER

We ourselves feel that what we are doing is just a drop in the ocean.
But if that drop was not in the ocean, I think that ocean would
be less because of that missing drop.

MOTHER TERESA

*I don't have to chase
extraordinary moments to find happiness -
it's right in front of me if I'm paying attention
and practicing gratitude.*

BRENÉ BROWN

You must be the change you wish to see in the world.

GANDHI

There is a calmness to a life lived in gratitude, a quiet joy.

RALPH H. BLUM

For me, every hour is grace. And I feel gratitude in my heart
each time I can meet someone and look at his or her smile.

ELIE WIESEL

When the door
of happiness closes,
another one opens;
but often we look so long
at the closed door that
we do not see the one
which has opened for us.

HELEN KELLER

No act of kindness, however small, is ever wasted.

--Aesop

THE SIMPLE JOY OF LIVING
FROM A GRATEFUL HEART

If you look to others for fulfillment,
you will never truly be fulfilled.
If your happiness depends on money,
you will never be happy with yourself.
Be content with what you have;
rejoice in the way things are.
When you realize there is nothing lacking,
the whole world belongs to you.

LAO TZU